longshadowfall

**The *Swan Song* Series**

*The epic of Gilgamesh,* (adaptation by) Saadi Younis Bahri
*Zenith*, Ingrid Calderon
*heshe egregore*, Daniel Y. Harris & Irene Koronas
*Future Awakes in Mouth of NOW*, Gerda Govine Ituarte
*Dirty Pretty Jaded Soul*, Timothy J. Morris & Christopher Sotelo
*Sapodilla*, Michael Rothenberg
*Serious Longing*, Jessica M. Wilson



**www.editionsducygne.com/swanworld**
ISBN : 978-2-84924-491-3

Michael Mc Aloran

# longshadowfall

Éditions du Cygne / SWAN World

## Foreword

"none unto/ ever unto blind bones for hyenic jaws agape no end till arbitrary reflect until…

precipice deliverance collide cauterize ache trace what lung foreign silentee…

breach dead stone purpose un-salve reduct cascade it-bitten brace long shadow fallen…

zero-tone eclipse ever-forage no not once still yet what as if to say some bankrupt cannot…

taste waste attrition locked once more upon utters vast no utters coliseum naught…"

this fragment of '*longshadowfall*' by Michael McAloran, already illustrates my thesis: that Michael in his writing digs out his writing, digs out all from underneath, to get to the essence of it all, which nowadays seems to be: nothing. writing is the medium with which one can reach these escatological esthetics, a kind of "anti-esthetics", seemingly the best as it eradicates itself while forwarding. of course, there are plenty of examples in other arts, philosophies and cultures too but specifically in Mc Aloran's poetry, poetry/prose, one finds a sufficiently radical expression of this black widow-like "literature fatale".

an "ever-forage" will go on and on in a "neo-postworld" or otherwise, prepostcataclysmic world, then, the report of it, as already that other Irish writers have spread out: Joyce and Beckett. as always in literature there is the factor of parricide and it may as well be them, to radicalise, which comprises what it also may be, radicalise by eradicating them. in my opinion Mc Aloran goes much further and also shows this new feature of "anti-esthetics", punk-esthetics, to gradually inject into what is written subtle dosages of toxins, which at once secure as dissect the literature which is built up while nowhere immune for the circumstantial pressures of "outside", and to withstand them is to not withstand them but let them in and whatever the fuck it is they're going to do: let them have it.

"cancel adrift redempt no drag trace awash with crimson surmount in ever-banquet…

eyes nothing tongue dead some pulse-bud symbiosis lapse no retort…

devours silt stone trade meat for nothing ever in bone deaf ever unto it says a glint…

words to carve out absenteeism/ it is stun less than ever-collision…"

in some manner, this is writing on the skin of the world and we find a plentitude of stylistic features with apparent overlappings with a small contingent of other artists, writers. there is the threatening "listing" method already a Linnaeus set up to classify the botanic world. yet this means here in literature an endpoint is reached, a "dead center". metaphorial, meritorial, economist, schoolist variables are already left here. in fact we're really standing on the edge of the world.

"eyes nothing tongue dead some pulse-bud symbiosis lapse no retort…"

this sentence, "sentence", sentence in literature theoretical aspect as judicial aspect, with its double negations, nevertheless conveys a richness which makes reminisces to Adorno's "Negative Dialektik"(1969) and "Ästhetische Theorie" which offered a dense, acribic language to decifer either or disencrypt, as he wrote in "paratactic patches" the imminent contradictions of which were no negative feature rather undistorted characteristics of "*the case itself*". perhaps "some pulse-bud lapse" still beholds a cache for remnants of a stash of coke could be held in but it is the "Tacoma Narrows Bridge", which, collapsed.

In the following last passus, (i loathe the term "stanza"), i will make some final comparisons of Mc Aloran's idiosyncratic art, poetry, poetry/prose, with other artists who, as i feel, show resemblances in style, un/style, approachability (or not, which i've learned from my own writings to not being a negative feature), inherent strength of voice (irrevocably), abstrahation of topic yet an accurate mappology of the endworld. Gertrude Stein, in her "The Making of Americans" shows in to the hilt that is: unto inintelligibility, in unbearable repetitive prose, "The Making of Americans" and it is a phenomenal book. what these writers do (Mc Aloran, Stein, Adorno) is an upholstery of the surfaces of the world, an inner and outer lining, following every crevasce, niche, gargoyle, pocked and lesioned area, they offer zone-floating, belettered and besieged and antsed up surfaces in either profane, sacral (but only mock-sacral), surfacial and perhaps superficial tableaux vivantes et morts alike. a funeral of the world as we know it.

Cioran, Céline, Celan all provide ample similarities with the writing of Michael McAloran. they stamped their work "fatal", "end", "deadly", "lastness", "lostness". "Of the nasty necessity of being born" (Cioran). "Journey to the End of the Night" (Céline). Georges Pérec's book "La Disparition" written entirely without the letter "e". I consider this to be part of the same punk-esthetics while it is an inner attack against either syntax as semantics (which in this particular book were kept, to make it all the more radical). so here "intelligibility" was key to otherworldliness. then we have the utter gratuity of Andy Warhol as to live his life as a nylon fixture inmidst the jet-set of NY. it is these rims, of life itself, which are being, not only written by Mc Aloran (et al), but also LIVED. I believe all mentioned, fit this bill of anti-esthetics. what rests, is the debris after the negations…

– Aad de Gids

# I

*…from in or out of/ in or out of focus of/ in/ echo strained vision in bespoke climb deft exhale/ resurgence ever/ flies upon denuded silence/ broke stone climb till foreign emptily/ from clot of edge an absent treasury/*

*collapses into speech cleft from heart laced with/ failure-adjust/ settles in valves of blank excursion/ settled shiv of eye's recoil/ out of focus unto reclaim/ unto/ passage from nothing unto blind-sighted ever/*

*here was once where null abounds/ in absent trace remaining/ bounty's dream lapse/ all colours absent smeared afar from focus out of/ of/ in-dense design nothing having charred all/*

*in-dreamt capacity/ breaks yes that it must/ collision/ fade to whisper no ever-reverberate/ embers/ atrophate/ nothing saying ever-what/ in suspend then absent/ in and out/ disremember/ focus never/ stun lapse/ until/*

*exhalation glint of drain of blood/ never of/ ever of/ yes or/ being what clap hands clap/ a mirror smeared with…echo-eye desertion tilt breath opulence/ nothing in/*

*forgotten of till unsung following after/ made null in breath of stun/ shaft closes/ lock-laughter echo dream unspoken/ unshadow absent/ light close disregard collapse unto fragrant not of yet of/*

*dreamt din in-spoke cascade blood ambulate/ strip no clamour cannot follow no/ not once/ disbelieve-shatter/ premise/ it what eye nothing blend/ in defecate of vocal lapse/*

*masquerade as voice/ dead tone fragment not a/ shock sharp edge/ record wall-spun collapse uninhaled sky shadow upon earth lack/ paper scissors stone/ edge/ sharp shock lapse/ opens unto vocal of unto/ fades then out unto/ fades then out fades in given unto/ recede/ traceless hours spent in/ echo's precipice/ not a/ blood reek of it/ motion bloom of no/*

*wind skull fled blood not a/ dense collect/ recollect binds trace absent recollect/ feeds upon what or/ vibrate/ dense die not a/ nor once before/ nothing/ dead lense adrift in/*

*collapse what shed if colour obsolete/ colours obsolete/ collapse then none or other/ other of then how collapsed/ yet still unto/ vocal unto/ silenced/ absent reclamation/*

*absent pace trace fade out/ skyline vocalized cannot/ reduced to approximate none/ lapse of/ as if to/ in-dead recession/ approximate/ fade out/ it cannot if unto other than only of/*

*traces echoes for/ neither nor not a/ zero forgotten it cannot other than or other…drains of/ collapses unto/ a breakage of bone oceanic/ traceless to claim/ eye's lack upon/*

*vault white dead-line head devours devour/ black light pulse utter utterance/ silenced/ all distance in or out of/ forgotten / unto/ forgotten unto/ nowhere bound/*

*sight sheared pulse dissipatory as if to/ unsung/ aptitude forgotten but once then of/ yet another/ in return to/ not of/ silenced of/ stray/ blight wind collision deft what/ aptitude/*

*sense violet/ drag terse residue/ again/ another/ sung for another no/ wilt light black/ shadow effortless consumed/ what else if/ cannot/ echo-din not another/*

*laughter-bellows/ skyline withstand yet adrift/ tidal absent/ corpus broke stone abound/ vital as/ what of/ impress in sand erased by/*

*trace of/ not a/ if or then what if another than/ silenced yes/ obsolete/ obsolete yes what if or other claim disregard/ nullified/ of forgotten effigies/ none what/ trace/ trace traipse/*

*empties out of sense what sense/ as if to...cannot/ pulse dense disregard in yet as if to/ ever trace of/ stone sense of/ ever-if/ non-if/ if-forgotten/ ever/ rots what of a lie it echoes no no more/ collapse of echo of/ yet resurgent yet unto/*

*voice yet rot unto/ embalmed vocal claim upon/ outro shaft shut snap/ another hour dies out/ clamour no/ rescind no not once/ once/ sudden as if/ (pulse beat)/ echo-valve shadowed none or from/ dead traces alongside breath bespoke/ catascope in roomscape/ in dredge wind wars/*

*collapse of all shears through as to / bites vein of if/ extinguished dense as of obscure/ (as was)/ obscurity/ tremolo beat of light erased/ dawn collision/ in reach lung lack/ none absent/ tidal/*

*sung aloft/ eye shock waste percept some obsolete devour/ fingers that reach for/ outro oblivion tide/ else what no...nothing crumpled into/ a ball of phlegm/ spat trace out into/ fissure present/ abhorrent/ what is/*

*not no nothing if or other than ever was if into or of cannot/ matters not yet or (smear of absent light/ words echoing through/ azure/ taste taste attrition/ strips unto the 'a's disappearance') strip sky palm open as was of before ever asking of/*

*silenced in and of/ it/ bit stun hollow tint/ reclamation no/ delirium/ lock of snare white resolve/ it is shit/ maggot/ fossilized nothing/ discarded teeth in wombage/*

*disrecollect unto future silenced...spark dread/ overture cascade of silence/ carved into word lapse vital/ unsung/ unspoken... solace echo no not/ asks ever of forgotten/ collapse into where grace devoured sunk spasm recollect/*

*interned/ bit bitten return unto from in or other than what of/ silenced in/ drain-light from forgotten pulse sarcophagus. . .dense die wind abort/ flesh besiege clear sharp trace across reflect/ in speech of/ from speech dead stop/*

*dense relapse abort foot-print once twice another if beyond/ laughter blight/ resound/ cannot...shrapnel close of wound observes from out of pitch/ black light/ suffocate of absent whispers/ expounds/ un-turn till lie's abstain/*

*no/ dead pelts scattered unforgotten/ break broken by nothing absent/ non else/ dreams a scar division/ skull-cap/ shadow's lacerate into/ unspoken none unspoken of devour/ absent majesty/ breaks as if it breaks it/*

*hands dead slivers concave conflex in broken unto ill/ remnants/ devoured colourings/ non-shadow stop as if but once/ clamour/ desire dead stripped in silence break light-streaked/*

*scatters solace non unto/ in-drift/ begs/ no/ yes or no/ of beckoning stillness/ forgotten breakage/ not once/ sound stripped out/ over-bearing light of nothing ever/ spent what nightscape/ remnants/ traces/ snaps bitten overture/*

*echoes lessened/ blight terse what winds to collect/ recollect/ abandon/ traceless flowerings/ abortive absentee of silent disregard/ broke stun of cleft seizure promise/ deft/*

*lung was once/ reclaimed/ offered up unto/ demarcate/ solace distance yet/ nothing/ none that ever was cannot/ merely in-dead spell/ opens unto final/ long stir desire of which emptied/*

*spillage of breath from lungtish corporeal/ drag-dense/ cast what yet/ no longer longing/ silence of absent longing/ fails in/ passage long tide/ if or any other/ breathen/ fallen/ not a/*

*blind-sight turn of precipice/ non-voidal/ night's eclipt/ drains just a little/ a little then/ shuts slowly shuts vault door across/ gouge of no/ yes or no/ expel/ for want of better disregard/*

*all sense devoured resurgent opulent fails in vague light's absolve/ lapse all else/ undone/ close of yet what will/ silence to become/ in a dressage of skinned approximate/ burnt winds carry/*

*obsolete hour expel/ shovel of ash into devour it cannot/ dead shadow break/ piss-reek/ obscene/ what skull what pulse devoured time no-thing be-ing/ traces foreign with fingertips obscure/ sidelong glimpse of defecate/*

*ennui mocked by further ennui/ final dirt as of silent/ spoke(n)/ sky-lapse dead dense white/ occlude light stammer from passage presence non-stir clot blood clot sequence/ claimed writhe in bit speech redressed/*

*aligned blood stone terse reclamation abnegate forget/ knows not what continues as if to/ shred absent sound pulse readily detach/ skyward empty stones thrown at glass houses/ upturned palm psalm dig furtive grave(n)/ stitch winds broke upon all fours/*

*exhalation/ knows not fever-dread till light collapse no trace/ awaits/ scar tissue belonging longing nothing of/ skull bite in rip blind solace/ fortitude/ reeks as it must/ vocal point of absent return/ ceases to be in momentary clause/ bites into/*

*dregs what matter/ stone cold observe/ steals aside/ trace ember lock/ open/ fettered/ dread light bled/ sun dislocate given unto traceless ever/ bind blind-sighted want/ abortive cheer/ sung bellows' tidal/ static outpour no wing mere bitter asking/ shattered surfaces/ obsolete blood-cold/*

*echo echo distance burnt traces/ delivered/ stitch of redeem/ as if what once where of what matter/ specious now what matter of it/ in-record of tide/ sky essence never azure nor black yet/ forgotten/ shaded/ what once/*

*waiting/ circumference dissolve/ of roomscape's dissolve/ cylindrical/ for/ better/ none forgotten/ tidal long foreign/ sweet dissolve/ absentee collapse ache of bitter shadow of bitten bitter/ holds breath seeks no no question/*

*driven/ axial divide non-driven driven unto...from bitter shard struck held asking of forgotten origins/ still yet projectile shadow lack/ upon/ not a/ or of in if/ unto/ through foreign magistrate/ dissonance/ sands burnt love disavowal/ spurious annulled/ ever if/ glimpse/ non-abounding/*

*less what matters claim yet if or other than if claimed forgotten in/ not a distance given/ out-flex/ (embers I what)/ nothing that ever was come to fore/ restorative/ cold death if/ silencing abort from/ dregs lest follow/ outstretch/ in-gleam what dream/ (dispersal)/*

*climb no/ ever no/ blind-sighted glimpse non-fashion...if scream dense nor of non-scream in if/ from out of if/ jaggered silence/ untold/ unspoken/ offered/ scattered pulse of long song final/ demise of what/ of a/ not a/*

*circulates driven obscurity of fleshed devour/ desire non-tread/ follows after/ closes pathway from out of unto skull/ recalls nocturne/ some foreign precipice/ absurdly/*

*collapse in-dream what dream abounding/ dense nothing/ nothing that cannot be other than approximate/ silence of bone whispers/ eats as if to/ solace snap-bone lapse/ desire/ speaks of desire yet what/ never yet or other/ once/*

*film drenched obscurity of veins/ tidal/ tidal all drenched reclamation no/ it exhales/ as if to...walls as if to warp inwardly flex of obsolete/ de-cries of wound/ percept then claim/ disregard/ laughter-wither/ expires/ waxen meat as was before/*

*absent solace cleft non-shrill/ collapse base recollective/ vomitous fade/ tremor/ full-stop what end/ what end of/ all colours jaded/ spent tines not a matter of it/ (spoken)/ dredge will winds no varicate/ breakage of breath lapse will redeemed of/*

*closer calling closer night's bone silence/ calls out ever-bleached turn of screw/ ave/ echo blank wall deflect/ riddled with/ occluded/ dense trace haven/ nothing to forgive/ (expand)/*

*expands from zero point of echoes abounding/ echo silenced/ turns bled from out of stitch-fever/ sought/ impact of cold stone wall's collapse given yes to be in vital no or other than/ respite absent claim/ vital nothing dredge silenced disregard ever-emergent/ never having abandoned/ crux/*

*blood fleck sudden ever lapse what wind/ (decide)/ opens up/ skull flowering outwardly kaleidoscopic colourings/ as if to kiss dawn's absurd light bethement/ cracks as if to say of it/ dream lapse arise/ none ever/ what of/ says what it will/ silenced all-while/ unsung/*

*not a/ devoured lung precipice incisor marks/ tears rent speech from collapse of emptily dragged from kick and scream/ steel eye dissipating/ obscure depth/ nuclei tumour blind light abortive whisperings/ circus spat solace/*

*glimmer tint of light revealed as...fingers itch for blade's recountive/ spinal/ depth will then out from out of spoken lapse until/ shit-reek of unsaying ever-yet until/ priced lapse from head till foreign forgot/ not a/ warped limbs of speech in retardation climb dreaming lest to follow as if to/ beleaguered/ blood-reek wounded lock dry earth in moist palm/*

*all climbing/ all forgotten/ dense else deflect it was said/ yet nothing in the ether collapse/ the either known...a doorway opens unto another/ asking of through prayers unfounded/ pulp beaten unto/ sequential/ silences stray wound as if to/ traces/ traces/ blind born blind seethes/ not of/*

*head-vast/ underwater skull/ stripped bare carcass kisses of dawn's elective/ (casts aside)/ follows unto ever/ posits nothing but stung barb inflex stripped flayed and on it/*

*severed limbs stone weight in gouge of asking/ it is not sun/ nor fragrant light nor dark it is the terse between one tension and another/ even if/ in if/ dries eyes it's just beginning/ wrung out/ crosses the palm with nothing / resplendent/ obsidian/*

*dense yes in it of none known of forgotten cannot other than in detrace/ abnegate/ drunk will/ curve of spine dies lapse/ amber ash/ cold bodies silenced grace/ silence abounding/*

*spit polish/ walks through walls without trace/ outflex/ polka laughter disregard it/ voluminous excise come to claim where none abounds/ echos dim/ fleshed will wind collision break stone collapse given unto driven until lapse begotten/ not once/ ice penetrate/ starry-eyed redeem lack attrition pissed upon/*

*none as collapse into/ desires that which has fallen yes refallen in scum flight terse opening up till sky retraced not once/*

*tidal ash/ fingers to trace what cannot be/ ever of not for/ shadowy absorb/ expels/ drinks down furious belligerent/ stealth rot in fossil graft/ voice as/ echo no/ not a runs aground/ into a gallowing of stretched abandon/ sways in wind/*

*breathes impaled/ no/ breath impaled/ detraced by mercury ever-given/ light fades out unto final static...dreamt lapse what forgotten ever-erased/ pieces together/ semblance dissonance/ expels/ yet silence ever/ eviscerate of breaking sky of decapitative/ final cards scattered/*

*naught in the raging unto/ given to precipice/ to base sounds nothing/ eye irrespective failure teasement of benign purpose/ as if to explore where nothing is out/ claustrophobe of jaw lock/ bound wind beneath surface of skin's blind skyline/*

*silence always penetrating as it goes / all said/ dead a long time down in dirt/ listen what for/ or of/ not a tune in head of mockery tune heard by buttress speech/ collapsed by/ mercury teeth bleed attrition/ what a/ exhausted possible laugh it off it will return exhausted/ shining into chasm fields of blood grass stun/*

*yet allwhile scattering of bone/ milk teeth/ charred remnants of words/ given to be wordless/ scarred obsolete/ carving away/ collapsed once more into a plethora of silent limbs/ nothing more/ nothing to be/ not a/*

*no nothing yet to be said of the none other than/ flash white skin/ intricate upheaval terse/ burning out...skyline folds filled by empty designs/ vocal burned clear of illusory breath outstretched/ prayers from non-depth/ base outcries unto silence* X./

*hand bitten feed/ elects foreign laughter/ bite as it chases/ dreams of forgotten night endless brute dense absurd lock spent collision extinguished eye/ ice upon flare of wound's pulse/ stray dogs/ hyenic conflict/*

*wordless as if to ask were to be delivered from/ dice will expounds/ vocal expanse shrinks to elusive passage/ placement/ not a trace/ passage dead/ open passage passage dead/ remorse of the fragrant skull ever evacuating/ based in in/ of of until/ as if to/ steel light reflect of/ throes final/ not a...*

## II

*...none unto/ ever unto blind bones for hyenic jaws agape no end till arbitrary reflect until/ precipice deliverance collide cauterize ache trace what lung foreign silentee/*

*breach dead stone purpose un-salve reduct cascade it-bitten brace long shadow fallen/ zero-tone eclipse ever-forage no not once still yet what as if to say some bankrupt cannot/*

*taste waste attrition locked once more upon utters vast no utters coliseum naught/ cancel adrift redempt no drag trace awash with crimson surmount in ever-banquet/*

*eyes nothing tongue dead some pulse-bud symbiosis lapse no retort/ devours silt stone trade meat for nothing ever in bone deaf ever unto it says a glint/ words to carve out absenteeism/*

*it is stun less than ever-collision/ brutal fashion subtle force astray sky-pelt echoes from out in else arise/ shattered glass gait traceless wordless given taken no never unto/*

*appears as such drowned parameters not a silent litany terse deft hands unsung/ smeared teeth bared what distance to evolve cold trace reclaim utter dark yes no again again/*

*ever what why what forgotten reclaimed without longing devour devours/ nothing appears blind white sheet light reeks of silence as known or another cannot/*

*intro clasp snare outreach cannot locked till film stray sound eclipt catatscope in-dreamt/ utter waste shred flesh filmatic sound echoing out from known unknown speech reclamation/*

*veins cold stun what cold kaleidoscope skinned lack unto nothing unto in blessed relapse/ sunk nothing* **it is a lie** *slipstream toothen glint in cavity of nothing yes or ever/*

*forgotten breath extinguished momentary desire clap hands forgotten lapse in eye brace none/ lock-bite dense strip-skin movement unto step no ever unto retrace broke bones harboring/*

*light melts down adagio darkness no absent one then another than silence ever was/ vibration yes walls yes laughter-shadow yet no not on merely silenced unto depth/*

*nor afar cannot will not forget-me-knots head of sand blood clot dust besiege/ in all dreams silence as reek silence hereto it dead jugular vision remains what a/ what/*

*unraveling membrane succor dead-end shatter fingers recoil exhale ever to be done/ undone in parry shadowy nocturne breach ember sudden to fall reappears/ disappears/*

*echo echo dull trace collective word gouge intoning night cannot unquantifiable/ till lung rescind abortive shadowed skin reflects unto dream foreign rapture tightened fist/*

*shatters yet no breakage bone light excavation marrow taste in acrid tint not a trace/ burns turns aside as if to jocular about-face breath skinned nothing ever other what/*

*there bitten extricated birthed unto one singular ashen promise all stepped alone/ scattered silences emptied rooms stillborn as black locked blood unsung unto what matter/*

*lays down dreaming dense eclipt all seasons devoured bitten dry from nucleus core/ savoured as if what collect bounty edge blades to sever obstruct cuts sensed awash with/*

*exit signs as if to say cleft pulse underwater skull stoked flame no given end until/ reeks once more blind-sighted digs up bones embedded skull-bile to eject collapse/*

*eats of it till lie resurgence fresh meat deprivation voice murmurs returns fades unto/ unto what climb utters as it should sky-depth lack till given from sanctions blood flow/*

*light slashed out in bite hyenic rise all skulled to all cascade till final X./ not tone un-word no not a word long fallen shadow draped across denude dark-light/*

*dreams in laughter-lie break upon till breath lock terse catastrophe silence therein shocks in/ scarred yes it begins from midway through retraces steps desire voice bled out resurgence/*

*not a in foreign distribute scattered ash upon gardenias undreamt unknown forgotten/ cylindrical promise not a till not a bitter blood in wilt thereof expanse/*

*mirrors from cold surface in tilt of light knock of cold trace desire resurgent cast unto/ dreams in else cannot erase lack cold coal features in blight cold shift/*

*paces about in catascope heliotopal eye in roomscape free from lack an instance/ bitter bones as if to echo oceanic emptily sets origami skies alight inhaling nothing but/*

*vortice till carousel drunk wild ash some intrinsic absolution close/ not a given lest taken roundelay collapse bit bite sharp cracked glass shattered form/*

*it shall be dark until as if to echo what from listless abandon all cards marked from out/ movement then abandoned from fever pitch shadowed fallen long bled out not a/*

*cold light breakage numb collapse un-spasm lightless soundless utters no not/ silent phrases bleak will wind none absolvation distances of ruin/*

*collapse final as if to say what zero ripped pageantry oceanic/ bites sting till sky pelt dispels fissure darkness as if there ever were any other outset/*

*winds nothing origin unknown taken from aside what mirror to shatter what of unto unto/ nothing in that some subtle deals death clouds barren vocalization speechless/*

*sound as if having if once more from out exhausted foreign absolute/ hyenic all along tears unsealed scars no not drained light breaking sharp bone shadow/*

*to fade undreamt in ice ablaze allwhile dissertation nothing no not nor no/ walls warp burn in drift of collapse into thy dread all stepped alone undone alone/*

*final to collapse in silence dreamt as if to utter were of any no not a nothing claimed/ why to ever-to what once from fragrance ashen clamour of some sung commence/*

*in spite of what song's adrift skies lack colourings naught-sheen upon tongue/ nectar dreams as if to final onslaught of benign flesh bone forget it forget it/*

*yet cannot be forgot in supplicate silence wracked to wheel's abandon in given accord/ rocking back and forth in pool of viscid whispers endlessly silenced yet never cancelled/*

*lies lies ever unto undone unto in glint tint of dim eye lapse shadow in other cannot other/ fails just as if silently chords severed light ground down to utterance dust/*

*less or more in absentia shattered frozen orchids all dreamt forgotten ever/ ex nihilo as in ever coagulate skull acid dreams beaten broken pulp blind silence/*

*slashed out till broken suffocate fever-pitch wounds to follow on along/ in breath-soaked idiocy disheveled colours denude dissipation excise/*

*cold colours cold dreaming in exigent shadow blind weight some given tantamount obscene what will closes ajar stretches out in striata-bite in gallows' shade/*

*breath-stung as if to echo what worm for closure tight-bind shit-streaked air/ maggotling of pulse-bud echoes echo-silent abandon fallen unto/ bitten drag collapse neck snap word mouth rock paper scissors silence/*

*vocal adrift unvocal clarify till dredge what matter done/ collapse/ casts out unto into nothing all parameters abounding fades unto not a/*

*laughter-spasm collision what till then bitten reflux expiration ever/ claims not unto in throughout vocal destitution silence(d) vapours/*

*all numb tirade blind sect abort cast out until fallen back upon till web/ resurgence fallen ashen graves unto nowhere bound aches lest nothing dim/*

*out-speaks itself blind barrage collapsed weight nothing left to claim/ dead light what colouring itself upon listless to shadowing cries out not a/*

*in blind bulb tears searches for ever-stoke empty prayers cold grave/ unto till end from purity lack none in distancia tears limbs from speech/*

*ill-lack ill-spoken silence reek seeks lest it follows kills what it cannot with clarity/ picks bones teeth-bound vultured kiss absence cauterized wound warp spinal/*

*blank sheet blood trace silence forgotte pared away rip tide discard/ sear-lights-tint shoveling up more shit than shovel tidal-oceanic/ vocal crossed up in silence speech devoured by silence ever was/*

*not a word remaining embedded cold collapse fragrant bile gathering in parch-throat/ voice unsaid it matter breath specious either way in block-light darkness/*

*churn of machinations bled out clamors that or other allwhile all stepped/ delirium of exigency waste sharp flesh to taste in death-kiss unto meat resolved/*

*trinkets for liquid eyes liquid skylines breaking from laughter-pageant echos out/ spies with eye-little all spun spun echo trace glimmer-bud exhalations/*

*in vocal damage seasons to expire from echo lock-dim tint alack none abounding in/ fades out echo echo tint reclamation scattered lights breathed absurdly foreign/*

*eye feeds it seeks it cannot all breath aligned strips skyline breath absurdly fathom/ paces cold light centre-roomscape colours absent locked teeth exhalation dragonfly/*

*lapse then absence force gesture vocal need dissipate clasp till scattered unto lapse/ once more back unto ever-in of naught space-trace obsolete cannot/*

*traces surface with fingers liquid fingers some ashen purpose collapse/ trace of spectrum in smear illumination reeks yet in none barricade none other not a/*

*steps a-nothing claimed rooted in non-pageantry juddering beneath breath exhalation unto/ till nothing left/ traceless desire/ blind weight scar tissue vomitous exigent exhalation/*

*exigent collapse in echonone vibrate sound feeding soundless broken break non-stir/ traces across it says what-in terse shear of breathe dense wound birthed unto/*

*it bound lung absent respite dense colourings absent focus broke stone filaments/ knots blind teeth till barricade collapse walls warp cannot only in wastage spat at/*

*exists in ever unto yet cannot trace blood glint in acedia spill obsidian/ eye lies yet nothing comes to fore brutal silence forage endless in it/*

*ever-endless cannot onward blood-flecked black absorbs unsound resounds/ in spectral tide occurrence screams out unto till ever wishful no nothing no retort not a/*

*it has been trace lock ill-mockery ill-disposed until traceless cracked valves expiration/ sings in accordance with/* **stammer**/ *dense laughter skull gleaming half-light/*

*dressage bound fingers mockery colourings meat skin bone ill-spoken ever/ broken laughter from out unto final winds counts down zero taste attrition/*

*opening out unto from out foreign chime will-wind echo-deep skin till protraction ash/ nothing further than belief disbelief shadow breath neither on nor scum waste broke-light/*

*flex-bend voice traceless dead lung in outro spills dead tomb intro from till speech accord/ wilted pageantry unsung devour collect subtle shard of bone collapse/*

*bitter marrow-fruits torn from skull's divide into from out all sense devoured nothing/ till venture in focus lack cannot resonate re-climb dense debris evisceration/*

*echo realm desire fallen from expire collapse sunk flesh endless landscape non/ viewed from distance prevalent colours cold as fresh final wounds closed scars to exhale/*

*opens up eye-lack bit-white eye sarcophagus till stretch sound wordless amber/ dreams some nectar distance reclamation no/ not a/ dreaming in midst of else/*

*some absurd light dreamt-dream vulture ever carousing flesh vacancy flourish paces no/ trace non-light expose no not on now ever unto onward now no nothing now stop cease pace/*

*beating in flightless wing's cavern echoing from end till end to ever-end/ long shadow fall embers ashes sands black sands it all falls nullity unspoken/*

*viper taste attrition sky-lapse pelt intrinsic blind collapse till vital edge no nothing for/ echo-glint exhalation specious wounds reek unsaying ever-silence/ silencing/*

*rupture headlong broken valves feel retrace till step abound unto where into ever ever/ head vast knows not cannot skinned silence flay once twice thrice absolute/ none/ not a/*

*lightless pageant some stone cold absence taken unto ever unto skyline/ trace dead pace lack splice perambulate cylindrical further further distance ever-never/*

*dead eye-lung whispers caressed brutalize skim no surface burrow deep/ yet depth in what some realm pummeling ashes choke spun on nothing more than/*

*it base attrition closure blind wound's appeal stark raving absent traipse/ returns unto silence breath meat rot saying none unto other than fixate/*

*meaningless a charade night teeth emptily spills unto woundage ever unto/ dressage final exigency skinned breath nocturnes beloved fallen waste taste attrition/*

*benign overtures fill spaces traceless given up from none no nothing more than/ lapse yes or no begun from nothing ever blind-taste unsung perambulatory silence/*

*un-sound collapsed vertebrae absent flowerings dead silences sands to caress/ voice devours vocal utter shit laughter long smooth surface of collapse in mirror's tide/*

*aches flame from out of some collision solid glass a view of black spun lack aborted-ever/ recoil in absence unto self-mutilation within to parry in-isolate in-reek in turn/*

*not a given distant unfathomable in-trace naught persistent drag tide's pull/ oceanic of which un-seeable merely some memory fallen ever unto dusts/*

*(bathes in…nothing far from…dead/ alive…far from…afar more dead than…cannot awaken…far from)/*

*tremolo heart-beat unto no nothing ever unto not now yet what in cyclical devoid/ spun heart circling sky once etc. eyes closed over in absentia cold frozen cadaver mist/*

*wrung knuckles shiv entropic sky pelt repeats cannot recall blind ashen blind absence/ in absence of fallen calling recollect shatte-red glass no a-dream cannot teeth bared/ eats all as if to/*

*collapse into/ ever unto not a silence flowing from permeation given/ blood lapse memory collect in suicide depth lock devour expels cannot/ sharp as if to echo blight collective no trace yester-fallen crux cavernous forgotten/*

*cannot be not a shit-deep in barricade spurious headless stretched/ as if to/ sparks death-design of vocal design not a sound nor trace tongue torn out hands barren/*

*sounds breaking silence merely barricade barren disclosure fading foraging no/ matters no all spoken collapsed into not a extent speechless upon unto nothing but/*

*sheared scattered remnants absent sound breath searing utter dark/ none/ scarred unto point bled out vacuous murmurs beneath breath absent audience/*

*drifts here then collapse intoned spoken as if it were or not a final ever/ it reclines seeks solace final throes scatters bound bones of membrane othering/ yet recoils once done into/*

*denude of intrinsic exigency span outro nothing/ all cleft reclamation what till in tint trace subtle taint dark upon non-objects ever-in/ (shredded carrion extricated bloody wings collapse in purpose tidal)/*

*blank screen pressed upon un-dimensional space absorbed form but one/ recalls in interstice unknown nothing shed it uttered vague shot of facial contort/*

*it-tint dim broke stone light ruminates yet it cannot dreams of what once/ not a/ tearing at un-sound dissipating fingers dead as cold toothen walls/ lapse long long/*

*long lapse long bloodless epi-centre amphitheatre/ not a/ stripping earthly shadows dry through unstrung extracted/ vacancy fission terror pitch in deep beyond blackening echoing coils inwardly/*

*in rapacious all shredded vicious light breaking from out from acid woundage/ reaps benefit of nothing beyond nothing in acrid taste attrition silenced as/*

*no taste for unsung corpsal seeks in blind white cancellation absolute/ solace in what in no further distance hollowed out pared out unto/ stripped/*

*skinned inwardly innards butchered unknown origin/ sanctions/ dry laugher spasm collective dead once manifold in dying retrospect/ searing membrane snap coils in once more given less than taken/*

*broken dust cascade intro speech given unto violent vicious in-cave rips to shreds/ seeks to utter nothing in from what collapse terse silence reek ever-in speech reclamation/*

*mosaic sky once now forgotten gouge in skull sense in wilting skull tears off splinters/ collision smashed broken glass form liquid porous not a trace remaining in within/*

*perceives nothing transient vacant blind blood warm merely to reject bloody mass/ shit/ bone/ cataract non-speech light flash scatters out illumines none abounding/*

*what will in raucous tide tidal collapse bitten stone blind over unto/ seeks sustenance in absence not a blinded by dark long shadow blight expel/*

*echoes in within extols magnitude perceives nothing embraced/ terror-reek solace of escape decay reverse not a trace of other than/ else absent catascope redressed purpose expels locks trains eye upon bleeds out/*

*unto silence returns no not unto in be-ing sharp shiv kiss blind nothing's trace/ unsung voice vocal wiped out traceless to exist in poverty beyond which/ vibration traces/ fade of out/*

*burn-bright-absenteeism dis-recollect/ remains intoned beneath/ silenced allwhile gathered speech inwardly extinguished/ silence without collision taint silence within voice-birth(ed)/ skeletal as/ fragrant as…*

*echo-tint cracked skin wordless breath(en)/ utter dark…long falling shadow-line…a carouse vacantly expiration/* **not a**/ *nectar gritted teeth/…/*

*spurious metallic evisceration blind-sighted in else/ none to lay bare utterance expiration hollow dredge non-speech haven test/ echo echo zero dim in glint eye cut to bone blight silence drag of fingertips across/*

*stings without purpose/ deflects without will/ it cannot/ movement without/ nothing/ acrid torn bitter reek dressage of final teeth etching still-birth blood to taste/*

*vacancy before sharpened blade/ seals unbroken/ not a/ seals up in wound of speech echoing distance untraceable/ stillness/ merely broken bones...*

# III

*...utter falter fall/ refallen/ falter utter none/ snap bone what/ blind solace bite/ faltered knocked from stray/ align/ what done/ till matter unto stray/ become what will ever having uttered once/ faint light filter through/*

*absence of redempt/ collapse/ un-bite bite mark breaks skin/ bitten all what dredge/ collapse resurgent knock given unto/ nothing/ dried bones/ how still to linger/*

*bitter aftermath/ untaste recollapse denuded hollow cleft what white/ sheared/ bled/ from outlook onset climb/ till marrow of/ fallen utter claim refallen/ echo din/*

*recollect relapse dread sky unfold of chariot breath/ in seamless break/ stun point/ knotted flesh marred silent prayer offered up/ for razor/ breath-like/ foreign/*

*recoil what matter dense around it goes some what or of to where-to-fore/ alack terse raises up to tear/ light-stream bloody solace not said once more/*

*again/ lock till nothing more from nothing ever/ walls warp yes less said of it/ so sung aloft breaks apart bone drift/ eases as it may till what/ or/ fleshed sarcophagus of memory/ drag hilt what tongue steel echo/*

*trace of blood white sheet grating none/ says butcher's paper wraps raw skull/ as flock escaping/ bitten in/ sodden with/ here or there what if till matter no/ matters not knotted reclimb of/ forget/ tossed coin sixpence drift alack/*

*returns endless dredge unfathom return unto/ skied-black colourless of voice/ naked twitch/ skinned appeal/ falter no/ again refalter fallen utter/ in skin of teeth/ in/ aborted/ why abort when fashion nothing tributary/ outward/ spits spittoon of nowhere left until/ breaks apart valves of feel/*

*eye/ all a-lock till here a no/ never once having/ gnarled fingers when nothing comes/ coiled in darkness fathomless a light in midst of suffocate of fist/ silently as/*

*till dead stone laughter collage of breath till heard dead dense/ what claimed/ reclamation/ scattered arisen what collectively nothing of preceding more unto/ till knock/ rapture/ fury depth/ it-spun cool entity nothing there/ recollect what passage point/*

*seamlessly ingrained/ lung/ ever in/ lung snap/ scar tissue of benign tears/ sight-lock/ breathless all denounced in or about nor from until white trace/ unsaid what sorrow done/ till lapse/ falter/ again steps forth what light lapse laughter/ template of scar division stripping (the) broke stun absence dread/ once sung/ retains once more/ echo warp till clear redone clotted blood never the twain to follow*

*sharp shock snapped/ from out of sleep till utter vacant/ recollects/ nothing more in none's inglorious hour/ dog shit in deserted alleyway unknown/ or thrice a trace/ some desire/ a broken absence heretofore/ eyed to sky reclaimed/*

*never known static other than/ till night or mourning morn/ in after-light/ blight speech a syllabus of unclouded eye/ lock till nothing/ clap hands absently/ retrace some subtle sustenance/ fallen/ faltered even/ passage from prism/ from prism blind/*

*none abounding a split in gait/ gash of teeth ablaze/ subtle as dry rupture/ lets dogs lie/ laughter all day long what is silencing this brief departure/ unspoken cleft as will reclose/ depth dug claimed/ from gilded atrophic/*

*marred by/ unknown in marred by nothing left to murmur of nor see/ again from naught till closure naught/ barren enclave of/ dredge no/ as if to having/ ill-unto it/ freely skull clasped to bosom/ crumples butcher's paper what (the) fuck/*

*here sung it is unsaid/ until/ screams out into black/ nullity ever/ void of what of/ speech lack of claim/ words dead foreign ice encasing fathom untimely said/*

*without till lapse again/ until foothold again/ no foothold/ absent foothold/ what said lapse/ fallen/ uttering of/ what of/ reclamation rips wings from fallen lights/ untold till go/ resurgence onwardly into dread/ further dread demarcating landscapes/*

*of broken glass/ till fleshed abandonment in nothing more an instance of/ unquantifiable/ reckless abandon/ nothing more yet echoes traces of/ skull brace clasp what matter fleshed unsteel to breaking apart till null/ still yet in die/*

*die cast rapture/ bone silence haven to/ from gilded atrophic/ heads rolling/ over and again in tomorrow's unto/ severed abandon-tide/ longshadowfall allwhile/ dense trace/ elected to this/ what matter/ not a/ speech reclamation from no naught-line/ in knock of utter falter fall/ refall/*

*empties from out of presence pulse decline it/ passage through liquid film/ gait pared away in presence passage/ film unto/ redone/ echo echo blind/ in struck strong blood reclamation no/ tastes/ bone shatters/ nothing claimed/ till claimed by/ not a sound in vice-clad breath of exigent/ colours laughter lack unsung/ in redeem of lack spill of dried wounds into cups of earth unfeel/ (this is)/ flesh it speaks alone in damage seasons/ celebratory pathway into soil's collapse/ foreign all and of all in/*

*about what said till lapse given unto trace refusal of stitch/ itch of redeem/ long call song/ presence pulse recline/ all day hours long/ (the) all of night/ passage through shattered fragments breath of some besiege/ it skull bit yet/ lapse lie what colours/ out of which struck forth into nothing being/ unstill/*

*yet of none/ in/ till clap of hands abounding shiv in throat stillness/ collision/ breath's advance a sly eye/ not a/ echos in it clamour lacerate/ desire cold shoulder/ kicked from fuck of light cast of another year/ all sought in dense derisory/*

*rage from out of fumes casts a desolate glorious/ silence in yet of/ till bone silences/ fists clenched/ tremolo blind/ teasing out/ emptied from/ unto/ settles then to ground/ in-lapse/ foreign lacerate/ bones knocked from no earthly splendour/*

*a cry in black light/ absent redempt/ sheared skinned blackened prism headless abandon/ skinned stretched unspoken/ in dead what once/ nothing to taste/ more shit than shovel/ more being than ever asked of/ yet none still itch glimmer of respective tidal/*

*eyes that gather/ climb yet falter climb redempt non-ask/ forget in midst/ colours flayed in vacant fading out cast winds from out of socket palm/ psalm/ expounding lightless marrow/ lifeless traces/ foreign unto ever-further no/ all sung what matter/ cast up to breath/ never until escapade/ outrospect/*

*as was said in/ beginning what/ skulled viceless heart minced with grief/ follows unto/ unto none where of or else/ clamour/ shredded once of less than other than/ dense till lapse recollect/ uttered/ fallen/ falter/ fallen falter fallen fall/ utter/ irredeem/*

*silences torn from acrid gutterings/ gutter lights bled sun obscene devour/ stripped carcass of breath in sky ablaze scarlet rupture/ headless alone yet never once/ held headless bitten trace into steel shutter vocal dystrophic lights/ in semblance taste sudden in outcry/ what tomb trace of obscure dreaming/*

*skin upon skin ruptured forage peal/ eaten of till depth refusal savage/ till spun clad/ in liquid speeches/ nothing from out of which belong breath shedding of/ null void all stepped alone remarked upon/ broken valves of distances/*

*what trace given unto/ dark ever to expire/ dragged through kick and scream/ of/ scattered sand upon blood raw flesh/ it eye lays me down it says/ foreign night alongside/ dreams cast out from wishbone in tragedia/ pared bones scattered upon/*

*blackened earth glimmer of dissent what scars to behold/ in Gloria of expelled all/ a sliver/ a chink/*

*not a trace left upon as if to breath what may in neveryet...all scarred unto till passage close of wound expulsion dread blind dragonfly excursions/ all salve bitten recollect/ nothing of till memory pulse-bulb rot a climactic endlessness/*

*stone graven outcry ruptured ever-vice/ it in of by till drag/ salvage no/ recollect redrawn in membrane sands/ oceanic climactic/ deal I what death comes in/ outstretched tasteless waste attrition text following unto gild/ irredeemed/ forgotten/ raw course till reek of earth as if to say no/ none/ emptily to gather as if of root belonging/ here song what skyline bled till forage never else/ in or out of culled speeches/*

*from what gather obsidian/ laughter-long a curved eye brace till gathering sickness/ gathers in light further sickness trace attrition foreign atrophate/ not a*

*gathered bone silences recollect dissipating none/ till in-drag following on from/ subtle cadaver light a tryst a foreign solace nothing more un-gained/ regained/ what sung all absentee sunken unto follow dead/ relights wick a stolen echoing/*

*all said/ unsaid/ uttered fallen falter fallen uttered dread reclaimed/ outro/ what dreams to unfollow/ shifting between one less than ever of/ what/ sung collapse into/ what dread/ motion unto/ wastage of/ in/ or/ dread neither/ follow breach of waver stillness of collected breath/ sought solace in other/*

*in maggot kiss restruct till absolution eye...construct of which given unto trace/ (less)/ as of gallows scattered confetti a broke stone sky/ flesh glimmer tint out of which until unparry/ meat till dim of closure/ so it/*

*bone silence dealt from out of fleshed veranda/ (close fist)/ this broken jaw/ ramparts scattered shells of being/ in redemptive no/ fallen falters falls unfallen...*

*again/ struck dead/ lapse/ again/ again unto from fragranced silences/ ever from/ carrion lights a deft reclusion rotting voice bled vocal out unto dissipating surface as/ it spun undone/*

*unto naught as was said as if to be forgotte/ impossibility of night/ till ruptured sky's resolve/ drag kick of scream into forage flesh/ what of/ echo's din/ aloud/ cacophony of unsung bleed/ shit for sustenance/ echo knock solace yes or no/ it bitten foray till laughter breaks all absent claims/*

*silence tomb what close of end/ opulence/ disclosure of emptied wound stir of/ collapsed vein of central exigent design/ in body lack/ arisen dead memory blight/ sucks dreams from silent tongue/ strips down scarlet silences through marrow ache/*

*desire what of yet settled/ given unto teeth what stammer damage light/ shines upon/corpse lit/ fingers itch for shiv unclosure/ wall's surface slides to barren floorboards/ ooze of revealed pulse-ridden meat/ locked lung collapse it bite reclaimed/*

*fallen yes unfaltering nothing yet or of/ until/ until all trace*
*forgotten solace haven no/ bit sting clear glass reflection desolate*
*sands stretching out into/ some/ foreign distance/ nothing more*
*to see of it unto/ what of lapse light collapse/*

*season itch what bite still damage unto nothing left but circus*
*exigency/ until until again/ lights extinguished/ shimmer of*
*reflective fades out/ clear cut steel tumbleweed discarded/ falter*
*fall excise bone nothing/ silenced over yet or of/*

*long shadow fall/ static/ dressage of toothen walls of burning*
*silences/ else yes what of till spillage dressed regalia unto/ what or*
*none redressed butcher's paper/ till dream what vortice/ drips from*
*silent fingertips/ said without/ until once more/ not a/ until once*
*more from haven breach/ a sleight of hand intro out of nocturne/*

*breath recollect it says yet stammers blind/ cold/ of where-to-*
*for/ reclamation depth/ until till pace about in circular*
*undoing/ scattered apart bled to shed blood weight/*

*silences to tread upon/ ashen bones as if to say what climb till*
*ledge unsaid/ as if to ever unto/ till clamour of forgotten lights/*
*all breathed aside/ knocked upon till traceless unbegotten*
*nothing/ echo tone of/ else in a mockery of flesh still yet in*
*unbecoming's hour/ flat-lined/*

*some final unbespoke trails off some distance parried/ eaten of/*
*alive alack utter unto aligned/ from (the) skinned all motion*
*graceless foreign semblance skimmed/ depth not nothing of it/*
*until replication/ seeks lest it be lost/ seeks yet ever loss/*

*in lack forever nothing of/ breath spoke dense air in-suffocate/ rapture fist broke lights arbitrary else/ lung what from solace clamour dead tone of/ listless following on from bite/ stun (I) laughter echoing skull's outreach not a trace/ abandonment/ seasoned traces/*

*eye-lock some other than bereft/ nothing left to claim/ as if there ever/ was where of bone haven tryst of recollect given unto trace redempt/ collision purpose/ not a/*

*it utters/ fallen sunlight upon a cold steel surface/ disembodied traces/ dried blood/ body vocal snared by/ given unto nothing more than ever fallen freely entity of waste/ freely motion no unspoken reek/ echos out what stun till shadowlight unspoken of…bitter lights to taste/ freely to burn of/ undone till spy eye lapse/ broken tombs of teeth/ suffocate's reclaim/ a turn of soil in membrane/ filament retraces/ gouges wound/*

*danse all days bespoke all bellow's tones/ suck of being outro vessel nothing of/ till emptily once more/ falter refallen fallen utter of bone silences/ nausea all/ settled to ground/ locked to/ fashioned of/ broken upon rocks of bleak finality/ oceanic/ long lost unto/ acrid laughter of/*

*drained of/ expulsion of bled once dry attained speechless none/ lest there be/ all sense devoured/ a plethora of bones chiming still-birth a/ denuded skyline breach taste waste attrition/ teasement of lapse air lapse redone/ garrotted*

*locked unto wind's reclaim/ whispers of expel/ not a trace of/ nothing more than/ hammer unto nails/ in cold light's revelate of undoing/ reduced to/ longing ever/ unto/ figurative sky peels back/ asked of some pupil reflect hollow earth skin deep until/*

*knotted root in dirt/ shit-caked fingers claw in desolate/ a redeem of bared breath/ opening out some reek in final ask what struck till settled/ breath redone not a chance ever spoken/ shadow-bite/ excise/ bone silence a tint of blood lays it down caress of shallow breath alack/*

*hollow ashes/ some semblance/ (echo I-dim)/ recollect I none variable stricken skinned/ vertebrae…of (the) one thing stripped away before (the) eye/ non-eye configuration/ stone blank/ not a/ ache done what given trace denounced vocal atrophy/ gait stripped of butcher's paper reveals nothing/*

*none/ remembers when some solace broke stone chalice of remark/ when none to follow on from/ I-steeled to reflections bite here or of what matter a/ bled outcried in shadow-veined skyline/ into un-sun it piss down blood as once did/ remembers blanked out/ mirror/ collage/*

*stripped down collapse/ inbreathe shift between one or another's eye reflect eradicated/ shoreline membrane skyline erased/ no not there in mind's closed wound/ re-open unto silence/ bone vibrate clear snap cut from ache redempt/ sudden in outcry nothing left to claim/ fingers pared away till silence drag/*

*drag of current blood smeared across bare white surface/ it tone to drag of sky pelt skin depth some acrid reek/ till end rise up cleave away/ cleft shudder snap/ lapse then/ some fashioning/ onward into nothing more/ outcried in lack skulled depth weightless sight/ outgiven closed fist a drag of/ entity/*

*shock-stone collapse echo echo/ tint dies down/ expel/ zero all's for unto given lack foreign lifeless cracked skull leaking ivy/ a-tearing of thorns/ else expanding/ rot in scum of night/ devouring all/ in glorious burn of night consuming all/ never if*

*pick wound I drifts I/ never of which/ cold vacancy of blade/ a trace/ a scent of nothing/ leaks foreign eye leaks liquid absenteeism/ through cracked shell meaningless/ spat upon/ forgotten not a whisper of bone/ a trace of flesh turned sour meats/ unsound/ dressage/*

*hour melts into another's hour/ sky pelt rots between the teeth of uttered once/ uttered not a trace of redempt/ collapses/ shears pulse entity/ laughter echoing unto/ not a/ it is a lie/ in turn of wheel scattered lights/ break not un-still overlay redressed shadowing/ inward/ outwardly unto nothing/ a stamp upon some distance stretches out/ no dice/*

*uttered/ faltered/ fallen/ redone/ again it says/ for what mattered/ for what never was/ stillness to gather in/ echoes/ traces/ aligned bones settling unto fall(en)/ of bespoke/*

*trace fingers across surface/ night's eye resolve/ dead lock/ bone weight/ nothing less than was/ utters yet cannot/ scatters tines of sound yet cannot/ in tint glint of glisten blood/ aches/ rescinds/ some silent distance nothing left to trace/ in redeem spat no blind furnace of/*

*nothing more or left behind/ outro excise/ dense wind hollow entity burns out unto/ expelled/ stripped purpose/ gathers in nausea flowerings/ it is/ said lack long in here or ever after what passage/ if then unto when closed wound spills decadent obsidian silences/ name etched in sands/*

*utters then/ cannot other than/ if other than/ lapse of then or what what haven not a trace/ obsolete/ foreign/ zero echoing in some collapse unknowable/ it bitten indent once more/ tears visage from skull/ vibrancy I-depth nothing claimed/ guillotine laughter/*

*spent breath in dislocate unshadow/ trading unto in out-fade relapse given unto none/ clamourage/ says again/ deaf ears upon which fallen/ it is sun all locked to bone weight this fleshed veranda/ skin of lacerate benign/ settled then to fall…spies what depth sudden in outcry/*

*this broken shell asking of prism pillage vapours clad in eye's resolve/ what weight what depth no depth mere vacancy/ before/ blade I-die/ unspoken colourings*

*base metallic a stretch of skin/ (again)/ contortionist dreams of silhouettes/ of shadowplay eats meat of eye-dim/ expels/ falters/ refallen un-spoken/ and oh so roundelay begin again/ in-zone/ bones no not nestling/ tears that (the) dead do not ponder/*

*in reek till trace collapse till foreign atrophate/ seasons beyond/ closes empties wound/ it is stone ashen purposelessness/ reek I-will/ scattered once/ thrice/ shadow's mockery untaste/ bites blade what in or till or of then or else become what dense what recollect/ it-eye sun/*

*fragrant says eye/ tolls/ escaping birds of blood into some vacant void/ struck out/ eradicated sudden as if to all unsaid/ murmured/ all as if or in what was given unto fore/ pares down further nothing more/ (wipes arse with butcher's paper)/ not a/*

*in-skin what will/ brace/ foreign ramparts of shed skins equatative longing of in reek unsaying none/ lapse-I what dreaming next/ unto/ into/ outro/ intro/*

*savoured less than sharp edge broke stone lies/a sheet-glass reflect/ bitten flesh in wound of fissure semblance of what once was never onward/ all final of what now/ if/ another's if/*

*motion unto rooted to in distance/ wings outstretched/ no/ flight dead burrow/ naught unto/ till cross one sudden psalm with silver eye/ minced pulse-bulb/ rotten/ undone/ fossil speech dredge of eye closure sudden in outcry/*

*trace desolate expiration sunk sung hollow overture brace of sky-pelt knocked from dead/ stun once/ out I in-forgotten/ process unto disappearance glorious inglorious/ scar tissue absent tears/*

*banquet yes to collapse in fields forgotten lifeless -1/ +2 or other of/ (the) reek fill lung/ from tissue bled/ doorway opening into/ as if once speech echo-trace all that was thought to be claimed/ no more/ nothing of/ dredged flung to (the) dogs/ scraps of inedible shit/*

*bone whispers/ whispers to caress silences/ outcry of naught beckoning rejection of/ goes not/ said without/ victorious no/ nothing of in ever what doubt as if to/ seeming to be what other wrenched from/ eyes torn out/*

*as if it were said/ solace rupture breath/ meat matter what/ endless/ remnants of/ faltering fallen fall utter of/ cannot yet calamity/ broke stone cold ice wither dreaming/ in-dreaming of/ what none I-ed to claim what longing for in/ longing from/ from zero point/ unto zero else nor fathom/*

*spatial sense of/ passage unto/ from lapse collect/ spied eye... utter here to lack/ lapse dread/ butcher's paper drifting shit-stained in (the) winds/ closes eyes sucked down into voidal distance no end to follow on from/ falter no/*

*devour lung eye from out of prism/ graceless to trace of/ outrospect/ collapse lack/ then let it commence it is said/ as if it never had/ forward unto that which is/ unto why no or yes no matter/ bled out/ carcass swing in kick of night's denude*

*and all that sings/ unsung/ falters fallen/ refallen ever unto if/ collapses not a word/ respoke as if from silenced/ in-dreamt capacity/ says no no nothing of till final edge upon/ so it is said what left upon/ till spasm upon surface deliverance what terse/*

*till tragedia non collision purpose sidelong glances view of sudden to expire unto/ still skinned less of purpose yes yet no climbs no height bone weighted/ silent bones resting in foreign as if...skin atrophate/ absent laughter echoing out/*

*stillness to close upon garrotted throat/ it/ what/ what/ solace of malignant tears/ I-drags what lapse/ play of (the) eye rapacious erasure/ turns inwardly into sharp red crimson ache/ burns black upon sight what endeavour/ close eye wound/ skull bare to barren skied/ rapture of reclamation barren hollowed out/*

*what lapse to follow/ final as/ stretches in cold blank desert edge/ cracked open/ unto/ seizure collapse I-drift/ spiral unto then or for/ bespoke/ silenteeism breathing/*

*clot of naught embrace/ jaded utterances/ not a trace given from out of sound/ foreign yet of eye yes or no/ slides/ never yes to fall/ other than/ nothing's claim/ what was once then dread/ scattered obsolete/ broke bones heartless/ scattered shale/ marrow's teeth/*

*it lapse eye lie/ spoke stun hollow echo/ again/ echoing again/ collapse of purpose dread alongside/ undone from out of which un-pace/ bleeds out/ collective/ rank trace in-breeze foreign nothing/ scattered shadows some pale elixir/ silence all about/ of some traceless within/ demarcate/*

*stone breath a body vacant/ cripple/ stung eye breathing of what of in or out of which to follow on/ I-lung I-/ what laughter of which to burn/ in night's pale theatre reflection of which will/ collapse/ stone now/ blank wall stares back reflective surface in which to perceive some nothing ever/*

*none-dance what/ locked to/ foreign ever to reveal/ immense turning of/ closes wound in finale sudden to expire as voice discloses none/ again/*

*again/ knotted fingers clasp inept unto/ for/ another what no other than in/ in this/ being in/ yet exit in/ not a/ breaks without feel/ skinned teeth abortive exile final final waste/ (we laugh we sing what joy to bring)/ silentia/ echo's shadow long falling/ in (the) growth of an hour/ lightless pageantry/*

*flies upon discarded meat/ maggot-lights/ pared down collapse I-din/ not a fucking hope/ silences of which bone dalliances/ forget-me-nots/ confetti laughter burns bleak/*

*un-said removal/ skull/ absent of/ bared blackly ruptured solace/ obliterate for what/ malignant hours/ (the)/ stench/ (the) rot from having/ exile of depth departed/ what closure none/ collapse wind breathless un-becoming/*

*till what/ what of/ a bankrupt cheer/ some struck eye-blind what drift spoken forth benign/ an echo once once only/ an exchange in none what of till naught/ bespoke/ silenced/ blood's laughter/ final flourish no/*

*carnivale/ dreamed hollow lights/ skinned purpose not a… skull's adrift/ origami figurine of flame/ till dream what night ever-night/ spurious/ (out-speak what speak till whisper's fade)/*

*what spill till overture/ close of eyes it's just begun/ it is said/ no further other than/ no further than...*

# IV

*…no never of/ never longing for/ yet somehow chokes stone dust in fathom lung abounding/ restless eye knotted clefts of teeth abortive unto spasm hilt/ locked underwater dredge/*

*what stun till paradisal winds a closure of redeem ever-lost no not a trace breath skulled unto/ unto winds that break from knowledge passive flung to rabid dogs/*

*blind blight a lock-held shadowing clasp-knife breathing severance erase not no/ not a trace skulk in or out of sound reductive fallen nothing uttered but for some trace desire for endless stone eclipt/*

*what pageantry motion unto waste/ to/ echo skin dressage of foreign nothing stripped to bone of rapture solace bled by dark/*

*closed fist gathered up proximity not a chance nor else given neutral bleed some trace malign etch of cold weight at vacuum's edge/ some carnage garden where/*

*skinned beknown given to outcry solace no undoing as it runs further into nowhere left to be some tilt yet heather roll in bleak blind air/ absurdly fleshed/ of yet/ ever-yet/*

*sudden in outcry traceless becoming heartless stone lapse…bared teeth eradicated/ in a smear of recollect/ such as is what of/ known of it forgotten not a trace ever of remaining breakage of what chance/*

*accustomed to some blind soil base rubbed into skin's reflect dice thrown yet yes yet mentioned ever of before till weight/ belonging lost/ it is stun/ none/*

*a swarm of flies in stitched mouth no longer gratified by anything other than a skyline evacuation of entity/ a savage dressage/ a birth a burst womb of silenteeism reckless tint of flayed bones wracking in pulseless glory eye unfathoming/ till foreign/*

*not a/ still yet in of what comes to pass will never arrive no departure from yet exit lights abounding allwhile/ taken by given some lax retort a lax recoil into nowhere having fashioning some breath by which to continue/ nowhere/*

*effortless recourse to some orchid blood flowing freely from gashed wounds here there from out of never close departed sudden in outcry given more than ever not/*

*no nothing more some semblance rot of eye rescind closed fetal breath bespoke forgotten blinded by tears that will not/*

*cannot/ closes in upon closed fist glass shattered breaking out from night/ nothing left to/ it continues/ it retraces/ casts only shadow's breathing lapse will else dead centre hollow edge gathe-ring up some absolute debris shed by intricacy/*

*bite derision collapse skull wrench all salve and surface a kiss of bled stone lights no further purpose/ no/ traces on in maddening steel eclipted madly skyline ripped from view by assassin eyes fixed upon less vengeance utters no unto throughout cold breath/*

*breakage from centre nothing clad with acrid pelts shed in some bitter unbecoming becoming/ in/ of knowledge that must cease on its own terms what once till sound subsides and fades/*

*it parallax till bite of dawn beneath an amputee skyline of said what said says on not a/ here we a/ eye-bite sullen inwardly some lapse in azure cheer head of dust of sand of blood of...fleshed abandon here or there from out of which what matter sunk stone head decide it says claims for final/ of final/*

*bread broken drying away nothing venerable no nothing claimed/ fallen/ as never was/ fallen steps retraced/ fallen steps retraced/ tread dead but once as if never having been other than what season's drift collision breath unskied as blood's metallic upon tongue/*

*given to cry out into some nothing other given having splayed this yet alone tearing pulse from bitten exigency/ shallow dread pierce of eye till lapse forgotten breaking bones in grind of magistrate/*

*feeling for oceanic in a black pool's rupture/ none/ it lapse what bitter sting haven of unstead till clamour dark what sense devoured beyond having breathed less than was necessary in a collision naught all flesh divided/*

*nothing more becoming fallen from depth's height peering out into some cold static abort of none/ it/ we/ eviscerate/ vivisected children rain-drenched some foreign light escaping from some origin upon a frozen hillside skies darkened by lapse death rising up as of winds to shatter all purpose close of door slams shut exposed eye graceless pageantry/*

*skulled lest of held in an abort of tragedia skinned to precipice denounced/ all lapse here or other/ again/ once again...some silence then breaking forth/ yet clamour of spinal outstretched in velvet sands flecked with blood (the) ruination of/ where one cannot go/*

*yet butcher's laughter yes gallows' laughter an ancient language of desire vibrating in meat-drenched bones an affluence collectively forgotten/ as pulse white bends in a holocaust of eradicate/ it is/ was is if unto is or of nor broke stone repetition forget forgotten/ flows ever-long/*

*as if to say that/ cracked knuckles viscous dreaming shadows a breathing else as if to say withstand where there is no longer any point of departure/*

*whispers collected in jaws agape hyenic laughter fragrant as rotting excrement blessed be some echoing chamber's lie of whittled bone silences cease to be as it forever says what nocturnes to behold/ collectively taken as far and from forgiving/ a taint of cum/ spittle/ sweat/*

*dry ice and an opiate syllabus counting out hours in pit illumined skyline as if to/ stylus blackened/ fleshed till dreaming of/ broken doorways an evisceration of walls peeling their papyrus designs in some rotting vagary no less some vacancy of smooth occultish absolute/*

*it done be in turning over in sleep this sleepless dreaming beco-ming other than what of it/ from sidelong side broken entity/ clasp weight of fallen taint a-stream in cold arthritic fingers no longer useful from out of some departure a given raise a shattered smile of bloodied teeth/*

*this scum ill-breath no longer of/ breathes because/ from out of birthed gardenias droves of forgotten prayers seeking shrift from shift promise no longer the or other than what if/*

*rounding out a naught from glimmer X. abounding in some semblance/ forgotten/ cast off spitting at some stone wind this wilting blood sarcophagus drag of here there or hereafter/*

*nothing's claim irreducible ennui pelt hung no/ no other purpose/ wrung knuckles some bruised calm of eye of which till sunlight's beckoning some further distance/ no/ not a/*

*burns off trace traceless echoing adrift in mindless vortice nothing ever other than/ stripped carcass of sound blinded by lights escapade/ forgotten/ fall what fallen of/ in a collapse of prism purpose prism failure some blood to taste a withered lightless/*

*intent driven from the beyond nor which artery climate/ sudden to exhale silver smoke a trace of desire/ nothing to see or other to move along unto lacks distance ever-way trace of malign feature blind eyes burning out of their socket graves where charred teeth chatter/*

*solace what sun a diseased railing against some other than/ an unknown pageantry of sense disintegration/ sudden to recollect exhalation of razor entity deals in death-cards/ empty traces/ nothing more than spelling it out words unraveling/ it/*

*what equates with soundless sound tearing some trace from vibration nights till dredged becoming else collision collide/ falter/ ex nihilo collide from out of none a face obliterated skyline chalice of bone warped lights lapse stillness pared amber colourless appeal/*

*outstretched arms that limply fall to some circus paradigm obsolete devoured sands in throat/ colossus shadowing of breath spoken dead once all bled some solace never unto ever what struck from opus lock an unturned key/*

*design desire breath spat out forage glimmer appeal till obsolete shudder taste climbs through cannot no way unto having other than of foreign silence beckoning/*

*till clear cut what cut clear glass spattered with lice bloody child exclamation mark stench reek piss faculty breathe some slaughterhouse irredempt/ falters none in none no nothing of till tilt tint of shadowing no longer dry clear in asking of forgotten/*

*knocking for some final some what or if given unto dreaming forgotten/ else collision rotting nothing/ exile of bleed/ a foreign disclosure discharge fallen wrenched from sacrosanct not a breath till worship driven from out of breath/*

*sunk eye in dog shit ever on display/ what lung eye given a trace of dead airs a fading musicality a dreaming next to follow further onward into nothing/ tapered goes some light's lapse all blood marrow taste collision nothing further to gain/ so says what/ once passed upon/*

*a silhouette a foreign banquet at which to dine alone for all time set in human meat/ bones of long speech desire lapses in and out of speech cannot through death's relapse an orchard of none/*

*spoke eye all dredged regardless vomitous unspoken words respoken not a trace gathering by winds origin of not a trace designed by edge to overcome collapse unto/ eye dredged lapse and then apart lung laughter on/ (to where)/ not on no ever-on into none no none is/ obliterate/*

*not a trace nor sound no nothing gouged out in instanced breath/ at vacuum's edge where speech treads gracefully upon terror's absolution/ obliterated by none corpus strikes out into nothing ever cold chase of echo-echo bleeds taste of discharge unlike blood opiate of desire/*

*a rip of cold flesh bone rupture hollow ashes scattered upon limbs that beg unto where nothing ever cold chase of echo-echo blood unlike/ scarred unto breathing stun dead flux abortive recollect shale struck bone flex flesh of disregard heavenly to touch winds gilded none lesser for what stone wind's design/*

*opening out unto/ reflex of else that will not/ no/ not a suffuse throughout what dead pulse rocking back and forth in darkness exhalations of final speech ever recoiling/ blending with collective traces no nothing non-voice a blend of tears and/*

*(regards with skinned eye)/ in frozen heart from out of damage dense accord a flagellate fingers gnarled cannot close over the warmth of limb upon limb gifted spasm held to burn what of it/ speech devoured lest sense be other than eradicated by purity*

*in a suicide of bitter teeth ablaze denounced cold earth tears dead do not ponder/ neither in or of obliterate concealed beneath each footprint in frozen surface/*

*cylindrical abase murmurs beneath breath trace of broke stone bodies clinging together as of shit to boot heel/ nothing there/ not a trace of redempt/ view is of outstretched vulture wings and the bleed of foreign silences for all time spent eradicated what songs from cancerous flesh to absorb no further than a lie from outset's chalice/ what sung we lung it is said/*

*premise no/ collapse into thy dread in a make of mockery cold shoulder of abort stricken skies streaked across in bloody streams a hallucinogenic upheaval throughout better repose of ice-dark-weight/ absence of all/ all shadowing/ all knowing yet not/ scar tissue of some unseen/ a/ not of not a/*

*snap bone itch however done collision echo-echo traceless what edge from which to strike into an irredeemable solace absence/ bitten bone eye light outstretched catascope where edge is vital sudden in outcry cries density a turning of soil over and over devouring nothing new that ever was nor will ever be/*

*so go words/ silence dreamt of never ceasing in conflict there its sense devoured by/ arbitrary lights break surface of skull's interior illuminating nothing more than ever was nor seen…not a trace/ voice in response collides with nothing echoing out in dry screams/ foreign whispers fallen at once to be eradicated/ nullified/*

*tastes whip as it expires/ back then till unto/ gathered in fleshed bones of ill-purpose opiate eyes close over nowhere left to see yet some/ still yet/ scar tissue yes peeled away revealing exposed eyes of lack and absence/ stone winds wilting blood flows from callused fingers unto vacuum's edge collecting bone whispers/ (seeded by)/*

*tumbleweed across desert sands of unseen mind's reflect/ in desolation's itch stitch of absence of redeem fleshed bones of within of illumined skull bleed of foreign silences...nowhere left from out of shadowing alack/ static/ black light/ severed fingers scattered across empty sands/ silent murmurs/*

*traces of memory fathomless an itch of redeem a vacant lot a vacant lot of blind bones bound in a pissoir's grace some piss-reek of/ blind shit devoured from whittled hands smeared across gait in mirror's reflect cracked eye-limb/ what circus dreaming cancerous obviation/*

*nocturnes of once having been dredged from weightless barren ovulate a recourse to blind sorrows sweet caress of deathly tears/ it or other than what given next to nothing turning in lapse collision fallen skies never truly fallen eyes devoured in oceanic apathy/*

*trace barren in skulk of fissure dread collapse unto thy dread one final breath to champion (the) infinite/ it we lung/ worming flesh of abortive symphonic/ bone break of body mount purity of some obscene devour a fleshed veranda silence breakage ever long/*

*untold reflect lock shadow hold breakage of bone eclipse explicit drive non-else given never having in or taken away unto origin non-said/ breathes yes desire closed wound an orifice dead centre solace break given to expire collapse in laughter's chamber/*

*breakage stun weight echo echoing from out of solace climb not a chance for living breath collide non-step retrace a marrow's overture/ shadowings across deserted concrete nothing left to give/ it was/ some night's detrace from out of stitch shattered glass deserted buildings some ever-night sky's blood pelt absence of redeem not a chance/*

*fucked frozen in or of or in come to fall(en) cracked knuckles of speech ever-silenced/ a broken asp silhouettes of speech disregard following on from trace wry sudden as/ it eye spoken no/ one singular growth/ be it/ no/ erased by writhing winds/ trace across distance no knowledge of before nor when in now/*

*following on from/ as if to serve where gilded purpose breathes one final edge/ till final sight closed in upon yet grasping nothing/ a word/ an approximate/*

*dead tines splendor of repeal given unto sacrosanct forgotten traces blind bones for giving of in sequence chatter still light in a wavering of sinew blight extended forgotten trace benign as/ here lacks dawn it say/*

*sound upon sound echoing in given lest to trace denounced forgotten lights a dislocate of emptily in nothing's realm spattered with semen none devours non-speech scars upon/ as if to other than recollect dry ice in a winter's longing traces closed wounds outstretched other than/*

*blind weight in given hope what other else/ (time to set aside blind emblems we deal in vacant psychosis)/ spinal outreach fingers grip obscene amber nothing of concede lest there ever having other shine black blood leaking from a breast in half light/ abounding/*

*no longer abort reckless freedom stripped skinned hung out a slaughterhouse erupt some other than a reek of human meat/ scattered unto/ cold concrete blood-soaked/ flies will gather nothing more/ as smeared teeth denounce all that was a trace of spit frozen in thin air for all time/*

*insert into/ fingers search/ none for all time ever to return unto blinded by lights devoured solace ever-cleft/ abortive running for further ground's desire/ dense vibrating walls cold as a cadaver/ nothing more of some final kiss meaning null and void sickness in-teeth to shine/ all seen outstretched/*

*vortice unbecoming widens view from one disclosure ever the separate of flesh and flesh barriers to demarcate/ not a breath in some sky stillness absence of murmuring of whispers silent as bone disregard/ till foreign final as what of/*

*sudden as if to unlock what cannot be other than reclose feeding frenzy collapse dried blood upon freshly slit wrists/ and obscure eyes that perceive/ dread in or in given to outcry in dark what weight what silence as of/ turning in/ shedding no tears for lost but stammer of (the) in/ being in/*

*snared/ fucking headless barrage axial grind death-willing jettison turning with ever solace division realm of some listless bleak what wind to pass throughout/ flogging dead hope of silent genesis collision trace of desire exigent blood peels away some skin depth altered piss for sustenance/*

*it associates with nothing more than break-neck speed a cartilage of tongues cracked skull roll over dances freely it says/ (dreams of dark are ours to genuflect before blind as gutted lambs in Spring fields)/ no measure to take and one singular purpose stone weight a bulk of flesh sung aloft in a polka wisdom of deceit/ lapse lie/*

*breach wind of eye's occlusion depth in what collide lapse flagellate expounds out through nothing of collapse intoned sudden as if to/ having ever blind-sighted broke bone light cast silhouette of some death-dreaming/ reaches for exit signs fades unto dissipate screen before which to/*

*nothing less or more given to exhale dead cascade forgotten never once yet in/ rigour/ shadowing all where there is none to grasp for solace dead screams echo-distance travail of specious disembowelment/*

*a burst abortion of rendered sever not ever erased from outset clear cut what done all said from beginning to end disparage… false wounds false earth see sky licking the oceanic from absurdly mocked to the edge of dreaming next what in forage what in trace undone collapse ever ever/ outreach yet/ for what or in/ of/*

*placement of desire what weight to bear/ a blood lapse sacrosanct in obsolete spasm emptily devoid of tears of/ broken lockets of smoke a gifted paradigm of traceless unbegotten following through given unto take from out of dredge what matter/ if*

*if belief of what matter of entanglement of silent smear a rip of flesh given unto traceless no hope candle snuffed out/ in moment between recoil and expulsion dread absent waters of abattoir nights/*

*long shadow of fallen to at water's edge a closed fist some longing/ for/ dread eye what lies from headless speeches nothing here to hold or behold some sudden as if to in or what sun's collapse dead light in a winter's collage/*

*genuflects before nothing in a vacancy of shit/ what light thrown to hyenic jaws a piss-reek solace collision death it or of or none forgotten in an instance hands seared by flame/ bitter overtures/ zero eclipse dry ice in a broken stylus claim/ becomes from with a flowering orchid taste seasoned climb never having ever once/*

*broken valves of feel in un-redempt of eye scattered remnants in barren soil collision breath-line/ where one is none abounding silver edge clay imprint solace ever bit stone clamped temple-skull from beginning out of edge a lie a shrapnel longing/*

*what was once then or/ if then then derelict/ spinal outreach in psychosial depth what blight to taste shed skins a breakage tongue uttering as if to say that it could no nothing/*

*barren lights a sudden red rash of no not ever if given to retrace/ it is sky it is some womb of teeth alongside given to devour its own nothing greater than wished for nothing more than should have never/ traceless idolatory/*

*un-trace of dawn's reclamation/ eye-see-eye what known mutilating earth's breathing/ some lapse/ some longing/ snared to bit and reach of given unto-fore in a lapse of in-dreaming/ where reek dusts vocal with bloodless appeal/ douses light what matter collide it-lung spits in face of all that ever was of if/ it-spoke and a dry your eyes/*

*debris to follow on from into further detritus sung aloft where die is to hollow known we longing in or which in other collapse/ mocks flesh that follows/ eye recalls/ peels back skin of teeth a reveal of carnage garden obsolete until/ sickness to dredge from out of slashed silence cleaving away as if there were any other than before/*

*dead in nail/ walls crumble foreign scent of tomorrow's asking of disregard sun will not matter lesser less than before what matter or dressage blind orchid/ azure blight taste waste of attrition emptily peeling film from struck eyeline's disregard a cold clear trace to swallow down itch reek not a/ fibrous absences/*

*it-skull scattered charred bones at vacuum's edge where nothing left to begin or from matters collide it-lung spits again in face of/ (eye recalls)/ still trace what depth/ nothing was bleeds out what said or of collapse eye-trace bitten hand pulse bulb locket asking of weight to bear some glimmer to reach for/ no/ nothing in or what/ such as/ breaks/*

*nothing other than another's other/ skin of teeth peeled back to/ to reveal charred rancid flesh/ fades out of a whisper longing of unspoken tidal in a gift of breaking tide of nowhere left to be/ nowhere having been/ bending with break of solace echo trace desire reflect some sunk stun tint in a dim reflect of fissure gait aglow what matter stings as it should/ bereft/*

*cast of then to an unsung devour/ nothing cannot vocal seeps into/ dried ashen promise/ dead lapse beseech you of you reflected in collapse unspoken whisper longing of (the) reek of (the) unsaying/ bankrupt pared skull vicious a winter gutter's flame/ an absent shadow arrives at un-point reduct in-dreaming of possible if/*

*cannot in-breathe lapse weight cauterized blood spillage spectral lights sudden in outcry given to for nothing other than bleed of fettered vocal atrophy/ viewed from an externus of never having once/ taken by/ breath suffocate a closed fist some nocturne's solace tide/ once then or of in matters closure nothing left of heretofore clamour-vibrate a fallen wind a skinned exhalation tremor decide what closure naught to seal all wounds never yet to trace/ it is/ no longer of/*

*neither worthy nor of nor exposed wound to scatter seed where once was arid ground/ having pissed one's last in abortive cheer/ finding no longer of in what matter burning out blood run dry effortlessly condemned to bitter shale an itch emptying one's guts non-literal through sheer teeth of maggot silence/*

*nothing's dread dead pulse from outset's screaming cold long shadow of fallen out-cry of sky's relapse traceless tint a hailing nothing echoing out from some exile's brutal/ construct/ and so on and on it parry to unflow wrenched from grip of bitter asp/ walls wombs of tearing fingernails from amber dawns/*

*absurdly broken glass scattered as of shrapnel in taint/ taint in/ echo-echoing out closed entropy some distance to trace long forgotten ever-clad in night's insensible features…and so forth it turns inwardly collapses dredged wind light closed seasons in some charred dreaming of final edge of breath to sever what can only/ fade/ undone/*

*in wind's reveal of collapse bitten to cherish a brief reveal of/ scattered lights as of warped limbs in a desolate of dreaming shadow's edge collision none in an obliteration of absent taste/ obscurely flexed night to fall it is ever-night in bleed of obsolete given unto from out of in or other than redemptive no quarter's tidal/*

*it is a mockery of wings burned to bare filament desolately collapse some taste of final rupture to bind flesh with razor wire hands dead nothing more to forage for/ beneath colours/ climates/ death's heads some absence here or of what sensed in outstretched limbs a broken jawline's exigency/*

*stone winds resurgence ever longshadowfall where nothing of reeks blind taste some solace no return again begin again/ in wind's reveal of collapse bitten as if to cherish pummeling absurdly lock associative/ till skull skinned screaming in an abort of flame settling into ash/ all sense devoured/ step non-step throughout as if to ever having to/ once/ about-face/*

*throughout non-step/ steps still widening horizon through bite of eye travailing non-depths foreign hallucinations/ a trace of blood streaking air silent silhouette of some dead belonging never to behold nor brace with tears told in some dialogue's embrace/*

*it stun why brace where nothing more than once sudden to outcry said once more/ the livid flesh silent cadaver's atrophic smiles erectile depths what sun to writhes in outstretch of time given to surcease/ skin to lack/*

*fingers smashed a gashed throat of vocal outcries/ where words disclosure bent upon some foreign yes or other than reveal it bitten flex/ barbarous/ kneels upon/ some fragrance no nothing/ not a/ in an overwhelming silence where none sleeps gracefully all else forgotten pregnant with doubt let it/*

*fade it other spoken fading lights/ static ever-static burgeoning/ as if to having ever unto passage through climb through flame reduct of lights blank light of/ gnarled skies burn in electrical storms yet ever of cold chill abounding/ spattering of cold blood upon shattered glass/ in a simulacrum of silent tongues reduced to severance not a trace of redeem/ nor need of/*

*it widens eyes a silenced ever-fading out/ gifted unto blind(ness)/ not a/ how less felt as if than other than ill-broken absent of sky collapsed eye-din what of no way nor other how to/ fallen upon a sword of acrid lights blessed be given meat's recoil/ blind shit as it was from some commence exhale inhale nothing more than other than through none's passage/*

*till skyline lung braced as if to other than as if to begin cold ravage/ all alack reckless laughter at one thing adamant…indefinite cracked eye leaking obsolete given to abort/ stun knowledge the nothing knowledge of catascope skinned to hilt of becoming other than no claims upon/*

*outrospect desire for one thing longed sought obsolete/ as if to endless in die rolled collapse over and other than again what again/ words flail of/ scattered remnants/ shrapnel chipped teeth of the unborn assertion given to exile's shadowing less and less or other than/ retort what will/ no longer a/*

*traceless abandon disappearance/ till other than/ at vacuum's edge where speech treads carefully upon (the) skin of terror/ excised teeth that run aground upon shores of bankrupt absolution/ feels for/ mockery-lung/ and breathe-block else exhalation +0/ it trace ill-tongue lights no/ nothing of collapse of vocal spread given to expiration/ following on from ever-savage/ of matter yes/*

*blind obviate of skinned purpose given to shadow's bite reclamation/ lapses as it does/ collapses/ intricacy of shit-stained teeth and black blood tint reflected in mirror's indifference/*

*what cannot be observed/ desire trace trace desire a vacant lot of burnt bones a vacant cityscape/ and so forth yet ending in/ no other in/ being in nothing more than sacred absent as before what else/ in-scarring static ever of/ dense devour knowledge of given unspeaking ever/*

*in desert tomes/ through/ echoes in where nothing in negates as if to say where it does not/ three blind mice ever the record/ bled out in effortless ecstatic/ maggot of pulse bulb to kill where splendor vortice falls to ground/ it* I/ *what of/*

*trace of what ever-known resounding in an absence of all other than or all effortlessly forgotten/ severed yes opened up till eye abscond from hilt taken as if to astray sunk nothing given of abound through viscous paradigm's occult/ gives freely of the slap to face that is never there/*

*yet felt in some wracked complex of better unknown unseen flowering dissipation/ yet fleshed as advance a bitten tidal over-mass upon/ blind weight and some circus dreaming clamouring for onset/ (forgotten the)/ sung aloft till dry of eyes it has just begun/*

*in cauterized wound given to seep solace in suffering consolation for all but foreign finalized/ dead lax/ seen unfelt/ not a/ chance a driven nail into nothing of (the) matter/ aloft pageantry descriptor nothing to display/ blood to yes/ taste forgotten yes recollected through passage present passage waste/ recoil eye lung/*

*taken from discharge some blind belonging some closing of eyes/ reaches for other fading out into some distance charade of betterment/ nowhere else/ never else or other than/ to tooth-edge/ hence echoing in cold chambers/*

*given to denounce from out of sheen some solace never other than some brutal fashioning crushing the bone echoings/ kaleidoscopic/ sought for longing in precipice given to exhalation never sought no other than furtive knock upon some sunk eye lapse of zero skin/ yet having seen/*

*blinded traceless disease of rescind as if there ever were any furtive/ inhales casts off this mortal enemy these cold dead hands that purchase further blood further carnage…unspoken yes lest to whisper from out of marrow's wailing in dark(ness)/ beyond a cross-fire of vision deduced bone whisper salve of the unclear devour*

*asking of as if to in about what claim as if to forget/ not a/ choiceless bounty lapse all haven stricken viciously from book what shadowing left where static abounds no gutted breath to love…as sought once in clamour lapse respoken turning into break light falter/ yet paring away/ time's passage given to mark the flesh as if it were/*

*pared waxen smiles of bloodied teeth no recourse for washing away silt of the malign/ outspoke nectar none/ climbing no yet getting to some height of none in an obliteration of it…seeking what what of till flourish final in what if or no restless devour/ hide dense as excrement/ bleeding out breath of unforgotten/*

*given to arise what drought from passage play/ nothing less nor/ as if to say that it/ nothing having been said/ yet wax lyrical it says/ some intrinsic landscape of bitten stone set against a swarming of flesh/ yet nothing to observe where vacuum's edge counts out hours in some deserted room of dust given to/ some song/ what lapse eye spies with grandiose/*

*a tint a tear there or other than no motion beyond some cleft desire for silenteeism/ having if/ no/ forgotten shores/ a peninsula of grave miscarriages spoken of in a vacancy of meat/ where noose is all yet nothing splendorous abounding shadow carves its gait into intrinsic sands/*

*some song lest yes we lapse in rooms in or out of passage/ where some crippled advance bestows upon stripped skin a menagerie of useless bloody meat devoured by bitter light/ crawl home speaks body's trace/ to where asks the further body lacking any retort/ obviated perhaps some stone glance writ in nothing/*

*words to lapse in or out of becoming viciously indifferent the eye...vocal and tongue torn from out of gouge no distance in trace unspeaking silences/ words cascading into some futureless abort tidal as a fresh-birthed as bloody as/ yet it sees/ it as/ it we/*

*no nothing a vocality of lapsed devour/ walls warped abandon in a catascope of breathing exhalation hold breath of which till follow on from other than/ in lapse till linger breakage bone break and solace interruption where no bone devours marrow's placement/ sunk spun a hollow echo-tint seeking out the coloured wind colourless/ colourless yet blind/*

*settling in to fall from out hyenic trace of benign given in malignant no nothing of unseen unknowable/ it bitten flays/ recoil/ in flagrant frozen from commence/*

*eye unshadow/ a stretch a gallowing landscape of suicidal intent/ having forgotten some brace trace of belligerent/ having forgotten other of in then not once caress that could not either way/ where stitched spread out into ploughed earth to sprout cold shoulder of all that ever was/ where traces devour/*

*skyline opens up till what lung dread of one thing only come to call knocking (the) shit out of verbiage seethe what tint/ all echoing lights flaying carcass emptily where speech descends as if to echo-say in tilt distance unbecoming/*

*naught speech depth ocular roving an anodyne circus trace nothing left of nowhere left to/ bitten shadow falls poisonous as in mirror's reflect of eye/ brace what bone done in fallen yest or absent lacking plumage breath what scum to behold in bitter sacrament throughout/ on it says yet no/ yet what/*

*blinded by lights stripping skin from purpose scattered from/ shattered of/ now tooth in membrane central to as if to say that it/ some foreign elixirate in blind speech some knowledge of echoing out essence of no marrow flesh blind no claps upon yet echoing of in barren shithouse/*

*from this/ ever-still yet in time mocked from and yet of in-what said collision yes collide spitting out plume origin of collapse nothing of it better than what ever-in/ of/ eye-shot-blood-shot-eye/ either or a movement unto waste the doorway opens out into further nothing of/ diseased words broken apart in midst of breath/*

*some soldered breath waylaid no echo-night-long-taint/ expulsion/ dread-locked semblance scuttling for cracks in floorboards/ escapes from out of which some corpus collect/ where season-death erupt what claim desire following on into crevice clemency/*

*meat yes writhing in a pit of acrid ash what have you as if to say/ in silence dread of one singular motion where to breathe is to suffocate upon further ice-clad nothing other than/ eye writhes what breath in skull lapse shadow on cast across a denude of hand left or right what matter/ in this/ be-ing/ not/*

*living in (the) not/ obliterated by none in lack of else what matters not a/ aching as if to say bereft of all/ a trace the expelled carcass of nothing more to gain of it/ words imparting nothing of no longer of being in/ in this/ deserted sky/ vision impaired the uncertainty of a future/ all's for unspeaking brushed aside asunder/*

*opening up a skull of division trace that clefts pulse meat bulb in severance to/ yet no not to/ murmurs of absent splendor/ shale of terse it spoken of what glimmer to wrestle with/ blank dead trace of spurious devour closed fist no nothing of in-dream/ rapture nothing/ excised/ furled lights and (the) beyond of.../*

*no retort/ cloud-burst of rotting words given in take what spell till eye upon where nothing gathers in its children/ all bite till wound/ itch/ collideoscopic/ blind trace of bitten lack expel/ little else but traceless forgotten in that specious light where edge is vacuum lights and sudden to/ no lapse/ naught/*

*candle extinguished from outset/ ever-lapse cloud spill of some else forgotten promise no no nothing/ in a trace of forgotten broken stone mask cauterized what spell till division asking of image given in mirror's claim/ some circulate/*

*knocked for sixpence no nothing of having been before/ recollect absence trace devoured by none in an obliterate of bask what words to follow on with-ever to subside from birthed unbelonging/ out-trace/*

*nectar of belonging ever-severed what clamour nothing held for more than an instance of insectal wings set free/ bloody razors of depth devour/ collision within marks (the) terrain what as if to wishful for it turns within seeks nothing of it that can/ flowe-ring dead senses cauterized as lung/ (where of the)/*

*all forgotten/ as if to make one's own in climate of exile where to be is to unbecome in the light of never to become nor ever have/*

*wound trace flesh/ broken now as if to echo/ unto/ brace/ now further now the winds to claim/ psychosial descent at/ (empty echoing)/ no no echoes either of to give yet in annihilate it speaks closes down blood of spectacle/ word's nothing chambers where promised solace all to cast aside/*

*as (the) abattoir expels its children taste of raw meat heart some bled accompaniment to/ so says it speaks it does not it cannot/ in failure adjust a burning insectoid filigree/ where taste absorbs and walls encase flesh veranda of desire unspeaking lights to taste/ it is said alone/ said alone yet foreign and unsaid/ undone/ (an empty echoing abounding)…*

*[...ends as it does not wish to have ever had/ commence then out or not what matter/ dries eyed spurious metals a vibrant bloody welt/ asking of some none till follow long shadow fallen/ it says yet lacks all sound/ rent flesh in scum divisive edge guttered night abort of fragrant none of it about/ or else what else not a trace to be seem/ strips bare nothing no no matter if/ in-lacerate of bedamned dried blood nothing drag of irrepent dragging the spinal affluence some solace climb to dream of exigent given to taste/ what wind/ make it nothing less than brutal not/ scarce rot/ drag of lights permeating skin in a drift pierce as one locks baited silence hovering in within not taken for less or more taste of saturate attrition/ bedamned/ lock in/ vibrating what stone said yes/ eye abacus/ brute flesh carving out into endless night what matter/ absence of/ strips shut down/ collision purpose scattered remnants nothing of/ till bite what ask/ prayers from depth departed sunk dead sudden/ collapse unto thine ashes/ a lung/ fibrous oxidate climbing transparent space elective drain what stun lack trace abortive none of lack displaced/ in seek of sun lights broken valves of having traced through laughter long given to expire/ skeletal/ traceless of eye what matter closed fingers fist shattered glass impenetrable sudden reject of/ biting down upon bared knuckles echo-echo traceless acclimatized/ there has been/ nothing crimson pace trace alongside/ till vacant light traces some accord what spasm senseless sense/ trace of non-percept/ glimmers deep/ in deep/ what well of liquid night of endless blood/ in-dream spits shards of glass into/ fissure semblant what/ it asks what spun colourless demise/ as if to say in murmur desert hyenic minced no solace it/ cold close till return of laughter traceless from some black origin unfounded/ lapse climb reductive/ speaks of dead cold harrow priceless/ aches just a/ not one/ forgotten dream pageant nothing no it closure/ as if*

*to say that in/ closure fist not a mark to remain/ settles to fall/ peels away skinned lights broken aspirate not a trace of/ broke stone laugh there is/ expels breaths as of shit/ bile vomit no breath for tomorrow/ (I/ eye laughterling)/ conjoined silences/ devouring words what frenzy to become…some foreign distance out of which collapsed purpose given to exhalation nowhere left/ to boundary cleft bespoke kill lack (lapse) kind what cannot be no other than bespoken/ nectar of eye sting breath colourless appeal a taste of bitter aftermath stings black worthless entity/ skinned for of in becoming nothing vacant seasons as if to echo dissolve in breakage point collision with no not a/ upon what stone sprayed with crimson broken valves of feel an abortive struggle fruitless as dawn's first shadowings/ emptily doorways weep into corridor/s of light's frozen cavalcades/ it-sting from frozen edge collapse still less than escapade given to fall asunder if/ lock weight and on it fathoms no/ bread broken through marrow's blind withering in traceless circumnavigate dissent/ bitten ill-light a broken jaw some tangential recollect emptily irredeem of/ no nothing of some sense through which or eye what sense collision naught in dissipate of waste/ as if to say/ dredge what will stillness gathering ache throughout cascade no not/ not a/ asks that it may what it/ is speaking what is speaking collision trace eject tasteless/ bloodless/ a neck snapped in emptily resounding as if to echo fade once more/ still yet what edge what silence breath some seraglio of excrement/ no words/ abandoned else a cold dark vacancy following through/ waste what stray opulent skull-depth/ intro out of speech wrung dry till kaleidoscope some breathless want/ of some longing that in/ not a trace of other than or if or in what spoken collapse I-breath/ eye-breath/ trace waste what love what closure fist no yet following on from/ blade between teeth/ all whittled down a sarcophagus taint tint in a lightless nothing/ spoken for as if for tomorrow/ not a trace/ in some following after laughter-lock some buried collapse/ lapse unto/ forgets forgotten that it has forgotten/ wrung out/ skins scattered vicariously across waste ground...lungs outstretched some bitter barb a stripped eye basking in sun lights/ alone is to best respite taken from onset's winds/ nothing that cannot be outstretched wings till die what once/ ragged jaw out of some out-pulse regardless fathom never spoken till clad stone break reflect cascade/ it-eye-what no more till barricade stripped bare in spurious silences/ spat out some final tongue into dissipating gait left trace of not a nor of in if no matter nothing says finalize/ night's fissure scarlet taste from a diseased mouth endless to touch beyond/ working bone against bone as if to say that nothing left demarcated stripped of tangents dry ice colours blending with tears given to unto some effortless demise/ it or other/ it what/ nothing more/ having burned all winds/ these burning winds deduced bone from out of faculty headless desire a given trace of some beyond forget it/ as one passes through another nothing there as if to/ broke stone fingers trace benign absence a dissipating smoke/ as if to/ having been no not for wastage not a/ clamour of dead light stripping the carcass of final tears lap them up for/ saken/ for no not a trace of there it all lies in pit tryst skull-depth snap-snap it is a lie/ mercury eyelids covering flesh/ here what collide what spun hilt dread laughter long as hollow/ not a/ strips violent teeth a mockery of being nothing beckoning in nothing's claim/ it-spun/ eyes roll back in amphetaminal lights/ not a trace of sky when sky is mind alone yet not a trace/ spoken of yet better departures given when lock is steel what driven else forget/ it is I-lie/ distances flung out into foreign realms/ no trace to touch/ what of/ none of it throughout/ a downward spiral staircase of diseased lon-*

*ging smeared with bloody excrement/ reek/ no end in sight taken from above/ no light by which to guide/ atrophic words cascading with flesh's devourment/ nowhere of some left to run aground/ where vocal chalice mocked by nothing claims what dim I-lack/ sunk white light of…ever of still-chase broke-spun lack till of measure/ gifting of eye what purpose flesh a* **wrang** *of meat a colossus breath still-born edge/ as of/ forget-me-knots shackled nonchalant skull deep what water winter water's edge/ steps to blood measurement distance haven cleft one singular purpose not a/ it still distillation breaking forth relapse of climb none from out of which to parry disclosed night disclosed/ crack what stone effigies detritus wastage of bone steel laughter prevaricate/ fucked frozen eye reclaimed stillness from which to escapade writ in lines cast by a windless full of blood/ it I-lie never once of trace desire nothing captured given unto causality driven terse/ etc./ eye-lack sudden to expire given of reject of purpose nothing left to trace where nothing was or if abounding/ ragged then in terse closed doorway in or out of/ nothing ventured nothing eye alone roving in said dark what dark/ blind arc ice to follow on from given to gesture/ dead all what some circus apathy/ dressage what will some stench of sickness given from retreat/ onward no/ flails off lack of purpose desire/ it we fallen/ drag/ yes another drag another bone/ another broke stone nothing amber lighted/ shadows shed across echoing out no nothing into which given to having forgotten from the outset of what if or/ dead we along/ scattered what longing gild of appetite an outstretched palm/ scum pageantry/ isolate in terse/ with we what if collective no nothing to obtruse skin of toothen walls no sense for tomorrow/ it is/ what is/ out of or other than/ dense die what collapse in cracked eye promise/ I-cannot/ what is of or in not a trace given to lack in dream sarcophagus collapse/ expired endless/ given* *to/ accord/ what sense then under-sensed beneath/ callous under-climate parasite/ blood-shot in bite of recollect/ deduced from bones what given trace/ it of/ what of/ not a/ in-dreaming posit of some lack what given violence/ aspen/ cold bait that once/ twice/ thrice/ echo-dim falling to earthen what spine no solace never to return…speaketh from form dislodged abandon cleft what climb/ subtle unto abandon eye's fieldline/ whispers from abattoir kiss ill-sensed as if to murmur bones of some unknown origin/ lapse all lack to trace from out of sickness given to dredge one singular motion ever to obscurity realm/ of distance clear azure perhaps some skyline only/ birthed all/ sudden abandon intro-speech eradicated not a trace where nothing can or cannot unspoken as before/ fields of lung no longing for abortive bones flies will gather nothing less as if to say/ some eclipse of endlessness/ in or out/ bled of what dead stun fields of atrophic reek shadowy nocturnes/ "dead fingers tell no…"/ absurdly flexed a catacomb of silence breathless expire non-trace in out or of/ here die it die eye/ we die young yet not enough/ better than what once was given/ effortlessly contained reclamation of none given to glow in unbroken aftermath/ I-we limb suck sand a broken coven a trace of flesh-meat nonchalance/ struck from what realm till opulent expiration/ skinned solace some glisten of liquid indefinable unlike tears/ not a trace where silenteeism reigns/ falter bled what other than/ if it we spoken nowhere left unto never unto/ dead centre centre flourish of nothing/ dissipatory expire sung from what left behind not a trace of affluence other than marrow's taint/ sunk suck stone spit it out/ "dead fingers tell…"/ skull yes this in butchery lights stripped does not/ escapes does not/ all dead what realms to touch forgotten arbitrary notion collapse eye-null-void/ coughing up blackened flesh non sense devoured/ seen last of what haven till of over than what stun vomitous teeth of some dead lapse longing for what end given beyond nothing there or othe-rwise/ it-stun what cleft lights repetitive edge/ colossus null and void we in/ reek of/ beyond shadow's mark a tint of closure nothing more than ever if or none sunk blind light of despair illuminating a thankless worthless space…]*